ALCATRAZ ISLAND LIGHT

The West Coast's First Lighthouse

AILEEN WEINTRAUB

The Rosen Publishing Group's
PowerKids Press™
New York

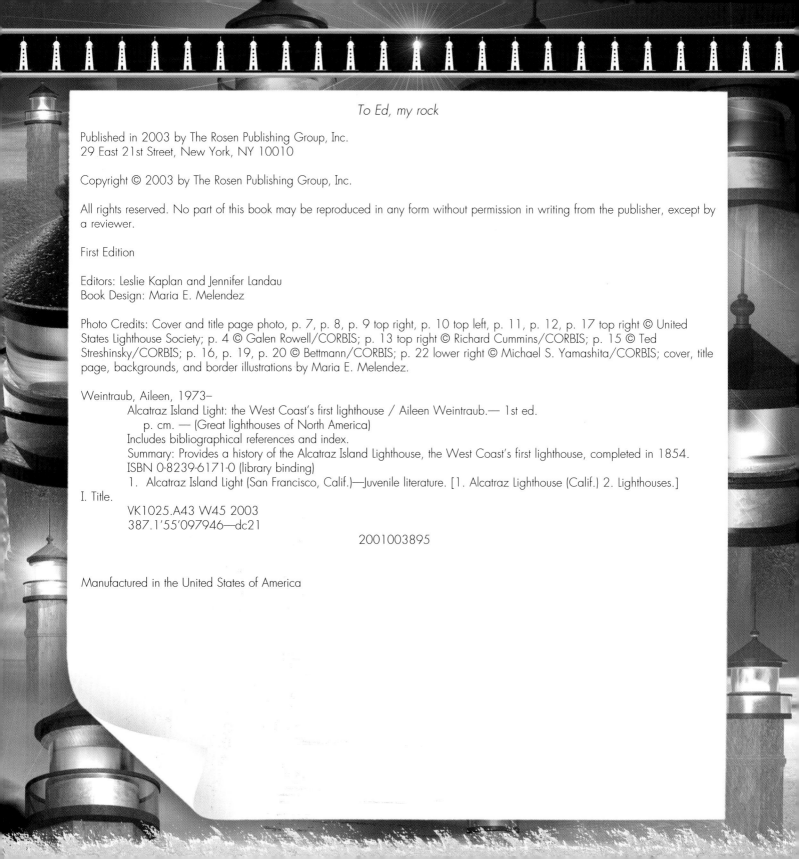

To Ed, my rock

Published in 2003 by The Rosen Publishing Group, Inc.
29 East 21st Street, New York, NY 10010

First Edition

Editors: Leslie Kaplan and Jennifer Landau
Book Design: Maria E. Melendez

Photo Credits: Cover and title page photo, p. 7, p. 8, p. 9 top right, p. 10 top left, p. 11, p. 12, p. 17 top right © United States Lighthouse Society; p. 4 © Galen Rowell/CORBIS; p. 13 top right © Richard Cummins/CORBIS; p. 15 © Ted Streshinsky/CORBIS; p. 16, p. 19, p. 20 © Bettmann/CORBIS; p. 22 lower right © Michael S. Yamashita/CORBIS; cover, title page, backgrounds, and border illustrations by Maria E. Melendez.

Weintraub, Aileen, 1973–
        Alcatraz Island Light: the West Coast's first lighthouse / Aileen Weintraub.— 1st ed.
            p. cm. — (Great lighthouses of North America)
        Includes bibliographical references and index.
        Summary: Provides a history of the Alcatraz Island Lighthouse, the West Coast's first lighthouse, completed in 1854.
        ISBN 0-8239-6171-0 (library binding)
        1. Alcatraz Island Light (San Francisco, Calif.)—Juvenile literature. [1. Alcatraz Lighthouse (Calif.) 2. Lighthouses.]
I. Title.
        VK1025.A43 W45 2003
        387.1'55'097946—dc21
                                                2001003895

Manufactured in the United States of America

Contents

Alcatraz Island Light looks out on the San Francisco Bay, the West Coast's largest natural harbor. The lighthouse is located east of the Golden Gate Bridge.

Lighting the Way

Alcatraz Island Light stands in San Francisco, California. This lighthouse has an exciting history that began soon after the 1848 discovery of gold in California. Lighthouses are towers built along coastlines to help guide ships to safety. These towers have a bright light at the top that can be seen for miles out at sea. The West Coast of the United States, where the Alcatraz lighthouse is located, has always been known for its rough waves, winds, fog, and dangerous cliffs. These conditions made it hard for sailors to **navigate**. With the discovery of gold, ship traffic increased along California's coast. More traffic meant that ships were even more likely to crash. Alcatraz Island Light, the first West Coast lighthouse, was built in 1854. It overlooks the narrow **channel** to the San Francisco Bay, now called the Golden Gate.

The Island of Pelicans

People first visited the island we now call Alcatraz almost 10,000 years ago. These visitors were the Coast Miwok and the Costanoan Indians. They didn't settle on the island, as it had no water or plants to support human life. In 1775, Spanish explorer Juan Manuel de Ayala sailed into the waters now called the San Francisco Bay. He saw birds roosting on an island, the one first visited by Indians. He named it *La Isla de los Alcatraces*, "the island of the pelicans." This name was later shifted to a second island. It is this second island we know as Alcatraz. While the Spaniards occupied California, the island was left untouched. In 1848, the United States took control of California. On November 6, 1850, the government decided to make Alcatraz into a military fort that would protect San Francisco from foreign attacks.

The island of Alcatraz is made entirely of rock with just a thin layer of dirt on top.

These plans for Alcatraz Island Light show the lighthouse keeper's house and the storage buildings where supplies were kept.

San Francisco Fog

The California gold rush in 1848 drew many people to the area, especially by ship. People came from around the world, hoping to strike it rich. San Francisco's fog made it hard for ships to navigate through the bay's narrow channels. The rough seas along the coastline caused many ships to crash against the rocks and to split apart. Often crew members and costly goods were lost. California's merchants begged for help from the government. In the early 1850s, the United States made plans to build eight lighthouses along the West Coast. The government sent men to look for ideal sites. Alcatraz was the site chosen for the first lighthouse.

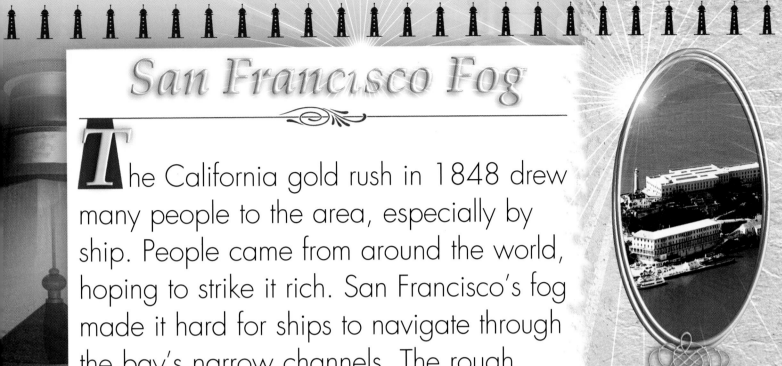

This view of Alcatraz island shows its lighthouse and prison buildings.

Building a Lighthouse

Alcatraz Island Light is shown here under construction.

In 1852, a ship called the *Oriole* sailed for Alcatraz with supplies and a work crew. Construction of the lighthouse was about to begin. It was planned that all West Coast lighthouses would look alike. The house itself would be one and a half stories high. The tower would rise from the middle of the house. A lighthouse keeper would live in the house and would keep the light working. All the towers would have spiral staircases. Buildings for storing oil and supplies would also be added to the island. The first lighthouse built on Alcatraz rose 48 feet (15 m) high. It was painted with black-and-white trim so ships could identify it easily. The lighthouse was completed in 1854.

This sketch of Alcatraz Island Light shows the building from several different angles.

A fog bell for Alcatraz Island Light is shown under construction.

The Light and the Bell

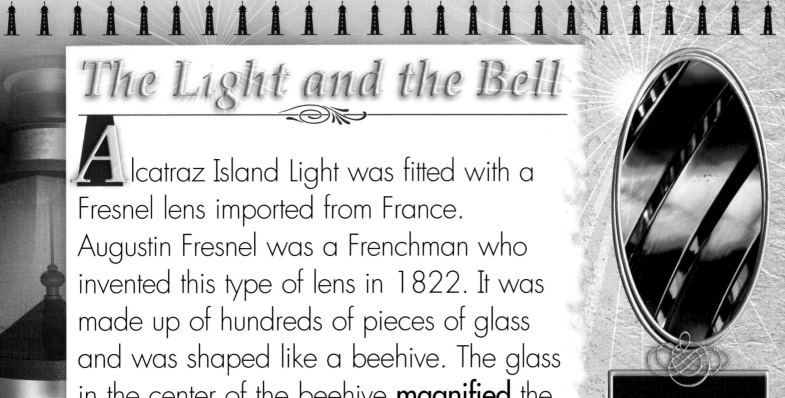

Alcatraz Island Light was fitted with a Fresnel lens imported from France. Augustin Fresnel was a Frenchman who invented this type of lens in 1822. It was made up of hundreds of pieces of glass and was shaped like a beehive. The glass in the center of the beehive **magnified** the light. **Prisms** at the top and the bottom bent the light to form a steady beam that was easy to see. The Fresnel lens came in six sizes, called **orders**. The first order was the biggest and the most powerful. A third order lens was **installed** in the Alcatraz tower in 1854. Ships could see the light from this lens for 14 miles (22.5 km) out at sea. In 1856, a fog bell was added to the tower.

Above: *Light can be seen reflected through a Fresnel lens.*

The Rock

Shortly before the **Civil War** (1861–65), the fort on Alcatraz became a **military prison**. In the 1920s and 1930s, the U.S. crime rate rose. More prison space was needed for **civilians**. Some of them were quite dangerous. In 1934, the old military prison became a **maximum security** prison. The prison was called The Rock for the island's rocky **terrain**. Alcatraz was a safe place to keep some of society's worst criminals. The island is surrounded by cold water and is 1.5 miles (2.4 km) from the mainland. Escape would be almost impossible. Only 36 prisoners tried. Most were recaptured, shot, or drowned. In 1962, three inmates did escape the island. No one knows if they survived or drowned. By the 1960s, the Alcatraz prison cost too much to operate. It closed on March 21, 1963. The lighthouse remained in use.

Prisoners step off the boat to Alcatraz. They could only have hot showers. This was so they wouldn't get used to the cold water in the bay and try to swim away.

A guard watches at the door while Alcatraz prisoners eat in the mess hall.

Keepers on the Island

The keepers of Alcatraz Island Light were always busy. They had to keep the light working properly at all times. When it was foggy, keepers rang a fog bell by hand to help guide ships. Eventually fog bells that rang on their own were built. These machines needed to be wound by someone every four hours. By the early 1900s, the keeper had three assistants. They took turns staying up at night to keep watch. The keepers led a quiet life. They had to follow certain rules, because they lived on an island with prisoners. For example, they had to crush all of their trash and throw it in the bay. This was so the prisoners couldn't make the trash into weapons.

Several West Coast lighthouses were built to look like Alcatraz Island Light, seen above.

17

A New Light

In 1898, the **Spanish American War** broke out. At the time, Alcatraz was still a military prison. This war made the prison population jump from 26 military prisoners to about 450. In 1909, the United States had a new, larger prison built to replace the old, wooden buildings that held the prisoners. Officials realized that the new prison blocked the beam shining from the lighthouse. A new lighthouse would have to be built. This lighthouse was 84 feet (26 m) high and had a smaller, fourth order Fresnel lens. Instead of a steady beam of light, there was a flashing light. This was so the light could be easily **distinguished** from city lights. The new lighthouse had electricity. Fog sirens were placed at both ends of the island. They warned of fog with a loud, sharp sound.

The jail cells at Alcatraz were very small, and prisoners were
not allowed to have newspapers, magazines, or radios.

Native American college students visited the island of Alcatraz in November 1969. They claimed that the island should belong to their people.

Native Americans Take a Stand

Between 1969 and 1971, Native Americans occupied the island of Alcatraz. A group called Indians of All Tribes claimed that they were taking back their land. A **Mohawk** named Richard Oakes led this group of almost 100 Native Americans. They wanted to build a university, a museum, and a cultural center on the island. The government ordered the Native Americans to leave. They refused. The government shut off the electricity and the fresh water supply to the island. Three nights later, a fire damaged many buildings, including part of the lighthouse and the Keepers' Quarters. Federal officers landed on the island on June 11, 1971. Only about 15 Native Americans were there. The federal officers loaded them onto boats and took back control of the island.

Steeped in History

Despite its stormy history, Alcatraz Island Light is still shining. Keepers served at the lighthouse until 1963, when it became **automated**. The Fresnel lens was taken out and replaced with a **reflecting** light. This light has a brightness of 200,000 **candlepower**. That's as bright as 200,000 candles. In 1972, Alcatraz became part of the Golden Gate National Recreation Area. People come from all around to visit the island, which now has a nature trail and is a protected **habitat** for birds. Alcatraz offers amazing views of San Francisco, including the famous Golden Gate Bridge. This island has an interesting history that helped to shape the state of California.

Glossary

automated (AW-tuh-mayt-ed) When something operates on its own without help.

candlepower (KAN-duhl-pow-uhr) The amount of light coming from one candle.

channel (CHA-nuhl) A safe course used by ships when entering or leaving a harbor.

civilians (sih-VIL-yinz) People who are not in the military.

Civil War (SIH-vul WOR) The war fought between the northern and southern states of America from 1861 to 1865.

distinguished (dih-STIN-gwisht) To have been able to tell the difference between certain things.

habitat (HA-bih-tat) The place where an animal or a plant naturally lives.

installed (in-STAHLD) To have set up for use.

magnified (MAG-nih-fyd) To have caused light to appear stronger.

maximum security (MAK-sih-mum sih-KYUR-ih-tee) When a prison guards very carefully against the escape and the dangerous behavior of its prisoners.

military prison (MIH-luh-ter-ee PRIH-zun) A prison where soldiers and people who are captured during war are kept.

Mohawk (MOH-hawk) A member of a particular tribe of Native Americans.

navigate (NA-vuh-gayt) To steer a ship through water.

orders (OR-derz) The sizes of the Fresnel lens that determine the brightness and distance that light will travel.

prisms (PRIH-zuhmz) Solid objects made of glass used to help reflect light.

reflecting (rih-FLEKT-ing) Throwing back light.

Spanish American War (SPA-nish uh-MER-ih-kin WOR) The war between the United States and Spain in 1898. As a result of this war, Spain gave Puerto Rico, the Philippine Islands, and Guam to the United States and let Cuba become independent.

terrain (tuh-RAYN) A piece of land.

Index

Web Sites

To learn more about Alcatraz Island Light, check out these Web sites:

www.cr.nps.gov/maritime/park/alcatraz.htm

www.nps.gov/alcatraz